Creating a Happy Retirement

A workbook for planning the life you want

Creating a Happy Retirement

A workbook for planning the life you want

Dr. Ronald W. Richardson &
Lois A. Richardson

Self-Counsel Press
(a division of)
International Self-Counsel Press Ltd.
Canada   USA

Self-Counsel Press acknowledges the financial support of the Government of Canada through the Canada Book Fund (CBF) for our publishing activities.

Printed in Canada.

First edition: 2013; Reprinted: 2014

Library and Archives Canada Cataloguing in Publication

Richardson, Ronald W. (Ronald Wayne), 1939-, author

    Creating a happy retirement : a workbook for planning the life you want / Dr. Ronald W. Richardson, Lois A. Richardson.

(Eldercare series)

Issued in print and electronic formats.

ISBN 978-1-77040-165-5 (pbk.).--ISBN 978-1-77040-924-8 (epub).--

ISBN 978-1-77040-925-5 (kindle)

    1. Retirement--Planning. I. Richardson, Lois A., 1944-, author II. Title.

HQ1062.R53 2013   646.7'9   C2013-903206-1

                                          C2013-903207-X

MIX
Paper from responsible sources
FSC® C004071

Self-Counsel Press
(a division of)
International Self-Counsel Press Ltd.

Bellingham, WA   North Vancouver, BC
USA   Canada

Contents

Notice to Readers

Laws are constantly changing. Every effort is made to keep this publication as current as possible. However, the author, the publisher, and the vendor of this book make no representation or warranties about the outcome or the use to which the information in this book is put and are not assuming any liability for any claims, losses, or damages arising out of the use of this book. The reader should not rely on the author or the publisher of this book for any professional advice. Please be sure that you have the most recent edition.

"OLD AGE IS FULL OF ENJOYMENT IF YOU KNOW HOW TO USE IT."

SENECA
4 BC – 65 AD

Preface

"Grow old along with me! The best is yet to be."

ROBERT BROWNING

This book is about planning a happy and satisfying life in retirement based on your own goals. It is not about financial planning for retirement. We presume you have done the math and know when you will be able to retire financially. On the other hand, you may not know how much money you will want or need for your retirement until you have decided on the kind of life you want in retirement. This book will help with that.

What will your life in retirement look like? What will you actually do on a day-to-day basis? More importantly, will it make you happy? Most people, in planning for retirement, focus on their financial plan but spend very little time on the question of what they want to do with their life in retirement. A 2010 *Consumer Reports* survey of retired people found that only 19% were "highly satisfied" with their planning for retirement.

Once you have the money for retirement, what comes next? That is the question we want to help you answer. There is no "correct" answer. It will vary from person to person and couple to couple. We considered starting with various examples of ways people have retired, but that would undercut the purpose of this book which is for you to discover how you want to do retirement in your own unique way.

We are not entirely satisfied with the word "retirement" for saying what comes next after a lifetime of work. The word has a kind of negative connotation, as if one is "dropping out of life." The word really describes the ending of a phase of life – the work phase – but it does not adequately focus on what comes next, the next phase of life. Retirement is only a doorway into a new life.

In much of Europe, people call this next phase of life the Third Age. In childhood, the First Age, the structure of our life is imposed on us by our family and by our schooling. In the Second Age, as working adults, we have more freedom of choice about the sort of work we will do, but life is still structured for us within that work framework.

In the Third Age, we have the freedom, within the limits of our income and physical well-being, to plan the life we want for ourselves. It is the time when we can finally say, "I want to run my life in a way that is primarily about what will make me happy." We can structure our lives in just the way we want, spending time, for the most part, doing only what we want.

This does not mean that life in retirement needs to be self-centered, hedonistic, and focused only on our own selfish ends. It could be that what will make us happy is a life of service to others, rather than a life of simply spending 365 days of the year improving our golf game. It could mean developing a whole new business. It could mean a life focused on grandchildren. The point is that we now have the freedom to choose what we want to do.

The challenge in this Third Age, after a lifetime of having our lives structured for us, is, "What do we want? How do we want to live our life now?"

During our working years, we have holidays in which we take time away from work to do what we want. Often, people think of what they do in their vacation time, when away from work, as what their life in retirement will be like. That may well be the case, but we want to suggest a more thoughtful approach to this issue. Thus, this book is primarily a work-book for you to do the planning for a happier and more satisfying life in this Third Age.

We have written it to help you think about your unique answer to the question of what next. It will also help couples discuss and develop a mutual plan that takes into account each partner's wishes.

In Part I, we raise some of the preliminary questions that are necessary to consider in approaching retirement. This addresses the context of retirement. It is about the larger social, philosophical, religious, and practical questions of what retirement means for you.

In Part II, we offer a framework for actually making plans for your own life in retirement. The structure is very similar to how we approached our own early retirement and what has worked for us and for others we have talked with.

You may not like the word "plan." Some people do not like the very idea of planning. Some of you from the business world may say, "Oh please god! No more planning meetings!" We hope you will experience this book differently.

Or you may want your life to develop in a more intuitive or spontaneous way doing "whatever feels right at the time." We accept that. We know that "we plan and God laughs" and that "planning is what we do while life happens." There is truth to these sayings. Things do happen that can completely wreck a plan. Not all our plans or every part of our plan will necessarily be lived. Life is too unpredictable for guarantees. As someone once said, the first point in Plan A should be have a Plan B. Clearly, for example, major health issues for us or our family will affect our plans.

However, we believe that having goals and planning how to achieve them gives us a direction to sail even in the midst of life's unanticipated storms. Planning is an opportunity to think about what is important to us in life, what will make life more satisfying, and how we want to go about incorporating those things into our future, whatever our circumstances.

Most people who have had successful careers have made use of foresight in making their plans for both their work and their private life. Whenever opportunities came along for advancement at work, one of their considerations was, "Where will this step take me? Will it take me closer to my ultimate goals or will it take me further away?" Having a personal plan helps us to answer these questions.

You may not want to do the "work" part of this workbook. Perhaps it will be enough for you to just read the questions and let them percolate in the back of your mind. Some people do their planning that way, and that is fine. We have found, however, that the struggle to do the work, to actually to put your thoughts into words and onto paper and then discuss them with someone important, especially with your partner if you have one, is extremely effective. It helps to clarify and refine your thinking and to make your plans more concrete and specific. Of course, you are free to make use of this book in any way you want or toss it in the garbage right now!

PART I
Thinking About Retirement

Chapter 1
Introduction

"Aging is not 'lost youth' but a new stage of opportunity and strength."

BETTY FRIEDAN

What Makes Us Happy?

The social philosopher and critic Eric Hoffer said, "The search for happiness is one of the chief sources of unhappiness." We agree. As a marriage and family therapist, Ron saw this over and over again in his practice. Clients would come in and say, in various ways, within varying circumstances, "I just want to be happy. I have tried everything. I have been to all sorts of programs, been to various churches, read all of the books, sat with many gurus, gotten married, gotten divorced, had children, taken a new job and I am still not happy." Ron would say something like, "Well, let's look at how you are living your life." Thus, the counseling process would begin.

The American Declaration of Independence, written primarily by Thomas Jefferson, says that people have "certain inalienable rights" to "life, liberty, and the pursuit of happiness." The author declared these rights in the context of not having them, as a foreign government imposed its directives on the American colonists. They felt they should be free to choose how they would live and what would make them happy. Notice that only the "pursuit" was guaranteed, not the acquisition of happiness. (The Canadian Charter of Rights and Freedoms on the other hand only promises "life, and liberty and security of the person.")

Most of us in the West have the freedom to pursue happiness. We do it in all sorts of ways, often without success, as many unhappy people will tell you. This book looks at the pursuit of happiness in the Third Age and what makes for a happy retirement.

As the Eric Hoffer quote implies, happiness is a by-product. We do not go directly to the Kingdom of Happy when we retire. It happens, or not, as a result of something else. It is about what other goals we have and how we go about achieving those goals. Goals, even when achieved, can be more – or less – satisfying. Many have said, for example, "I want to be a movie star. Then I will be happy." That is their goal. A few people get there. Then some of these discover they are still not happy. Other people with other goals in life have achieved them only to discover, "No, this has not made me happy."

Some have wondered what Jefferson meant by "happiness." Years later in 1819, interpreting his own phrase, Jefferson wrote, "Happiness is the aim of life, but virtue is the foundation of happiness." He might have had in mind virtues like kindness, love, forgiveness, hope, zest for life, humor, gratitude, temperance, courage, justice, transcendence of self, aesthetic appreciation, self-regulation, perseverance, prudence, and good relationships with family and friends.

Whatever the particular virtues, Jefferson was asserting that happiness depends on people's character. We build character through living a life of principle. Happiness results from and consists of the principles we choose to live by and how well we can hold to those principles.

Many people think of happiness as a feeling. They seek good feelings from experiences, from how much they earn, from where they live, or what sort of house they have, or neighborhood they live in, or who loves them, or who they are married to, or how many people are on their Facebook page, etc., etc. These things do not make us happy. They are external to who we are. Ron's therapy practice was located in one of the wealthiest parts of Canada and he saw the evidence for this truth every day. It is what is inside us that counts. Happiness is a matter of being, not having.

If we depend on other people or outside circumstances to make us happy, it will never work because it will never be enough. Someone asked one of the first Rockefeller tycoons, "How many millions are enough?" The implication of the question was, "When will you be satisfied?" He replied, "Hmmm. Just a few million more." Whatever level of income we have in life, we often think just a bit more would make us truly happy. Not so. Look at how many lottery winners are still unhappy.

If we focus on what we do not have, instead of what we do have, we will be dissatisfied. The grass can always look greener elsewhere. A *New Yorker* magazine cover showed the intersection of four backyards in a suburban neighborhood. The four grass yards were slightly different shades of green. Standing in the yards, each owner was looking over a fence to the neighbor's yard, with a look of envy for the other's shade of green.

Do your plans for retirement focus only on what you will have financially or materially, or where you will live, or what you will do, or are they inclusive of who you are? A happy retirement is not a commodity one can buy and sell. It cannot be bought in a store or a program or even produced in a book like this.

Who you are is the key. Only you can decide what kind of person you want to be and define your goals (within the framework of your marital and family relationships). It's up to you to decide how you want to live and relate to others.

Attitudes Toward Aging

What does it mean to grow older? Everyone has a different response to this question but, in general, there are two types of responses. The first is that growing older is a downhill slide into the grave. This is the sort of depressive response that any of us can recognize and may feel from time to time. In the gym one morning, Ron asked an older man (meaning older than Ron), "How are you doing?" The man responded, "Well, I got up this morning; and a lot of people didn't." This is sort of looking on the bright side of the slide.

The other attitude is that aging and retirement is an opportunity to develop new knowledge, skills, relationships, endeavors, etc. We have all heard of 90-year-old marathon runners and others with incredible physical abilities. We know people who go back to school and get a degree or who teach others about what they have learned in their career or their avocation.

We do not want to be oppressed with stories about the amazing feats that people achieve in their old age and feel as if we should be doing this as well. But we do need to have options for how we live in this stage of life and not automatically limit and shutter ourselves within traditional attitudes toward aging. There really are new opportunities for a new life and much of what we can dream about (certainly not all) could well be possible. Ron decided after retirement to take a ski instructor course. He had no intention of instructing, but it was a chance to learn new skills, to use what he knew already about working with and teaching people, and to achieve something he had never thought possible before. It was a proud day for him when he got his instructor's certificate. Another man we know went to Africa and trained as a big-game tracker, again without planning to actually get such a job. A former teacher went to Kenya to volunteer on the staff and do fundraising for scholarships for girls to go to high school. She did that work for six months of the year for many, many years. We could go on and on with examples of creative and interesting retirement lives.

A number of books offer advice about healthy aging. Most of them are very good. One of the best, we think, is by George E. Vaillant, M.D., called *Aging Well: Surprising Guideposts to a Happier Life from the Landmark Harvard Study of Adult Development*. Vaillant has been involved for most of his career in the study of healthy aging and in this book he reports on three longitudinal studies that followed people's lives for more than 70 years.

Previous studies of adult development tended to stop around the age of retirement – at about 65 years of age. They did not look at how life continues to develop after that point. They tended to say life was going toward decay and illness from this point and not worthy of studying. Vaillant and a few others have discovered that it is just the opposite for many people.

Vaillant offers the best evidence of what makes for healthy aging. Part of what he does in this book is to chronicle his own changing attitudes toward aging as he interviewed most of the people still alive in these studies. Early in the book he quotes Betty Friedan who, in her seventies, wrote, "We have barely even considered the possibilities in age for new kinds of loving intimacy, purposeful work and activity, learning and knowing, community and care.... For to see age as a continued human development involves a revolutionary paradigm shift." (*The Fountain of Age*)

Vaillant's book reports on three groups:

1. "A sample of 268 socially advantaged male Harvard graduates born about 1920." This is the study he has been the most involved in personally over the years, publishing a couple of books on them earlier in his career. He was ready to stop writing about them or studying them once they hit their mid-sixties until a member of this group challenged him to go further and not give in to the stereotypical view of aging as a downhill slide.

2. A group of "456 socially disadvantaged Inner City men born about 1930."

3. "A sample of 90 middle-class, intellectually gifted women born about 1910."

We refer to this book more in Chapter 6, but here is a summary of four of his findings on retirement and aging as a rewarding experience.

- First, people kept adding new friends to their lives. If study members had not added a new friend to their lives in the last ten years, they were not usually aging well. What this meant is that they had not replaced social contacts at work with involvement in other activities that allowed new friendships to develop.

- Second, they knew how to play, whether it was competitive activities like bridge or some other more physical activity that got them out and about in life. The focus was not on "being the best" but just being involved in fun activities.

- Third, they were involved in a continuing form of creativity.

- Fourth, they had a pattern of life-long learning.

Vaillant quotes one man (in his 80s) who typified what he meant about these four retirement activities.

> *In the last ten years we have made a great many (40-60) new friends, about 30-40 of whom we feel very close to. We have been welcomed into a play reading group, a bowling group and into the local yacht and beach club. These folks brought food and flowers, etc. during my recent illness. Several came over voluntarily to perform tasks that I could not do such as getting stuff put away when the hurricane threatened and getting our vegetable garden ready for winter. We have felt extremely close*

> *to these folks for four to five years. I also think*
> *that I am closer to my brother and sister-in-*
> *law and to my wife's brother than I was in*
> *1990. (pg. 225)*

Other research is bearing out Vaillant's findings about the new life people discover in retirement. This is not based on income, race, or social standing. The successful retirees are across the board. People at each socio-economic level do well in retirement along with those who don't do so well.

In addition to the four areas of growth above, Vaillant lists six personal qualities that he found in the people who were aging well. Almost universally, they:

1. Cared for others

2. Tolerated the "indignities of old age" with grace and accepted their dependency on others as needed

3. Remained hopeful about their possibilities in life and were realistically autonomous in pursuing them

4. Had a great sense of humor and found things to laugh about nearly every day

5. Got sustenance from memories of the past as well as engaging in new learning

6. Maintained intimate contact with old friends as well as family

In an earlier report (in the 1990s) on his study of Harvard men, Vaillant said one surprising result was that the men who had the best relationship with their siblings were also the healthiest men in his study. This is not a surprise to us. Good family relationships, or improving relationships, are a sign of the kind of emotional maturity it takes to age well. Those who go into older age still feeling bitter and cut off from other family members generally do not age well, as Ron often observed in his therapy practice.

The Characteristics of Happiness

The nature of one's character is central to the question of happiness. In the first ten years of our working life, over forty years ago, we lived in the inner-city neighborhoods of two middle-sized cities in the eastern United States. We lived among and worked with some very poor people. We ourselves were in a low income bracket. However, we were happy and knew many happy people. We met people of character who were not depressed by their relative poverty or run down by their living conditions. They were never going to have the luxury of planning a life in retirement in quite the style of most of you reading this book. However, because they lived a principled life, and had strong virtues of character, they were sure to be happy in their old age.

Certainly, having an adequate level of income is one factor in happiness. We cannot discount this. Studies indicate that as a retired couple in the U.S. moves toward having a minimum annual income of about $50,000, they report being increasingly happy. After that level, the relation between income and reported happiness slowly begins to level off.

Other factors that research indicates are important include a sense of meaning in life, having good relationships with important people in our lives, and doing things that we define, in our own terms, as pleasurable. Some form of spirituality seems to be important to most people, but many atheists report high levels of happiness. Happy people have high levels of gratitude, live hopeful and optimistic (rather than cynical and pessimistic) lives, and engage in the challenges of life around them, rather than withdrawing from life.

Altruism is another characteristic. Many of those who report being happy seem to have embodied some version of John F. Kennedy's famous statement, "Ask not what your country can do for you; ask what you can do for your country." In other words, they are not looking for people to do for them, but they are looking for what they can do for others. This is one aspect of good character.

Character, Happiness, Planning, and Retirement

It might seem that we are making retirement sound like work. That may be true to the extent that being a better person and living a better life requires work. However, the payoff of happiness and satisfaction with one's life makes it worthwhile.

The psychologist Erik Erikson, who studied the human life cycle, described the time of retirement as a psychological battle between integrity and despair. One aspect of retiring is a tendency to look back at what we have done with our lives and ask, on balance, "Has it been a life of integrity? Can I feel good about my life?" If it has not been a life well lived, then we are tempted to despair, feeling as if we may have wasted our lives.

In the Third Age, we are still creating our lives. Life is not over. Part II of this book has some life review exercises. Doing these will give you clues for how to proceed with your planning in this new part of life. Of course, this stage of life is not simply about looking back. Retirement is a transition to a new beginning, but what you have done previously will have a great deal to do with what you do next.

We are our memories, including the unhappy ones, but we are still creating memories. We learn from our previous experiences, even our failures. We do not want our lives in this new age to be a repetition of previous failures, but a life of wisdom and satisfaction. We are still writing our story, and the question now is, "Where do I want to go next in this story of my life?" None of us knows how long that story will be, but it doesn't hurt to plan for the longest time possible, keeping in mind the possibility of declining health or income in the later years.

How to Use This Book If You Are Already Retired

If you have been retired for one or more years, how has it been? Have you been living the life you once imagined, or has it been slipping past you much faster than you expected with few of your dreams realized? If this is the case, what has kept you from living out those dreams? Are there still things that you want to do but have made no specific plan for when or how you will do them? Are you as happy as you could be in your daily life now?

If you are fine with your answers to these questions, then maybe you do not need this book. However, this is a chance to rethink how things have gone for you. If you are not happy with your answers, this book can definitely help you to rethink your approach to this phase of life. Do the exercises just as you would if you were approaching retirement for the first time. Then, as a result of doing them, you can think about how you are going to change your life now, if at all.

Chapter 2
When, Where, What

"Retirement isn't the finish line."

UNKNOWN

Longevity Is Our Future

As we all know, the baby boomers are marching into retirement in record numbers. The boomer generation in the United States (born between 1946 and 1964) consists of 78 million people. The baby boom in Canada was even larger proportionally, with 32% of the population falling into that age group.

Apart from the obvious implications for the social security systems of these countries and their ability to support so many people financially, another major implication will have a significant social impact. People are going to be "old" for a much longer period of time.

When the United States enacted Social Security in 1935, allowing people to receive a government pension at age 65, the average male life span was 62 years. President Roosevelt, who initiated the legislation for Social Security, died at the age of 63 and his primary staff aide died at 55. It was an accomplishment to make it past age 65 in those days. Today, the average life expectancy for men is 78 and for women it is 83. However, once we make it to age 65 our life expectancy jumps to 83 for men and 86 for women; and these numbers are increasing each year.

The percentage of people in the population over age 50 in 1900 was 13%. In the year 2000, it was 27%. In 2020, it will be 35%. That year will be the peak in the retired boomer demographic explosion.

By 2026, 1 in 5 people will be older than 65. Today, 1 in 9 people are expected to live to be over 100. In our grandparents' generation that figure was 1 in 500. Compared to even our parents' generation, we are likely to live 20 to 40 years after retirement, and these are likely to be vital, active, healthy years.

Where retirement once signaled an ending to active life and a move to the rocking chair (or recliner), and then the hospital bed, and then death, today it is the start of a whole new phase of life. This stretch of 20 to 40 years of probably healthy living is unprecedented in human history. People used to work right up to the time they died. The new norm is to live into what was once considered "very old age," with many of us living until age 90 or 100.

There was once a fear, even a hatred of old age, that someone called gerontophobia. That view of life past 60 is changing. Many more people are eagerly looking forward to this period of life and counting on their life in retirement becoming something new and different. The negative images and stereotypes of aging are dying out. Ageist attitudes have less currency nowadays. People are less convinced that youth is the best time in life.

All of this brings our question, and the point of this book, front and center, "What will we do with that period of time?" We are on the frontier of a whole new age of living.

For example, there has been an explosion of adventure travel for retired people. People in their 70s and 80s are doing things like jumping out of planes with parachutes, climbing high mountains, or backpacking through South America. These things were once considered only the realm of a few young people. One 78-year-old woman recently made it up to 28,000 feet on Mt. Everest. Lois cross-country skis with an 87-year-old woman. People are going parasailing or skiing well into their 90s. A ski area we go to sells ski-lift passes for a group of people they call Super Seniors – those over 75. They sell quite a few of these passes.

Even if not doing dangerous things, older people are traveling and engaging in leisure activities that were once rare for people of their age. In a *New Yorker* cartoon a middle-age couple are watching TV, and the wife says, "When we retire, I want to watch travel videos." Road Scholar, a travel and educational program for seniors, changed its old name (Elderhostel) because it did not want to give the impression of being just for "old people." Many people are going back to college and pursuing academic studies that they have dreamed of for years. The "golden years" has taken on a whole new meaning. It is no longer about the "sunset years." For many of us, these are the new sunrise years.

When Should I Retire?

The first question about the timing for retirement is, "When can I do it, financially?" Next is, "When do I want to do it, emotionally?" Finally, we ask, "What will I do with it?" As we have said, we assume you have figured out the answer to the first question. The next two questions are intertwined, with the third question being the primary focus of this book.

As young adults, Lois and Ron thought very little about retirement. We did not even ask the first question. We simply expected to work "all" of our lives. Then we had a year-long sabbatical from work and a whole new vision of life opened up for us. This was in 1985 and we were in our forties. We travelled in a VW camper van for a year in Europe and loved it. We fell in love with leisure travel and the kind of active life this opened up for us. We met a number of other people in Europe that year doing just what we were doing.

Even though we both liked our work and felt that we were making a meaningful contribution to society, as well as having decent incomes, the result of that year off was that we began to plan for early retirement. We lived on only one salary and saved the other. This meant we lived a modest, somewhat frugal life. We had a vision of something different from a life of work. The material sacrifices involved to get there were no big deal to us. It was another 13 years before we actually retired, but our life in retirement became our focused goal.

Retirement Is Not for Everyone

Most people, like us, are eager to retire and do it as soon as possible. Other people put it off for as long as they possibly can. Of course, a great many people do not have a choice; they have to keep working to have an income to live on. However, we know people who still go into their office at 80 and 90 years old even though there is no financial need to do so. They never had that dream of retiring and doing something altogether different with their lives. They find their work life so satisfying and energizing that they cannot imagine life without it. They may be like Michelangelo who began his work on St. Peter's Basilica when he was 70 or Frank Lloyd Wright who finished the Guggenheim Museum when he was 89. We say more power to them, but it was not for us.

Ron was surprised to find that when he was able to retire financially at age 55, he was not ready emotionally. Even though he looked forward to retiring, he felt "obliged" to continue to work for a few more years for the sake of the counseling agency where he was executive director.

Lois definitely wanted more time for outdoor activities, but when Ron retired, she waited another year because she discovered she was hesitant to give up the social connections of work life. Once she had sorted out how she could deal with this, she was eager to stop being in an office all day.

The point is that there are emotional issues as well as practical ones that enter into this decision and no one can say, "This is when you should retire." We knew there were other things we wanted to do with our lives besides work, and we did not want to wait until we were too old to do them.

Another factor in deciding when to retire is how your timing fits in with your spouse's. A difference in age as well as different career paths can mean a couple is out of sync in their retirement years. Although we have a five-year age difference, our retirements were only a year apart. It was partly seeing Ron have more "play time" that helped Lois make a decision to stop working. Many couples have a greater age difference or perhaps one has already been out of the workforce for several years, so their planning is more complicated. The basic principles, however, still apply to both.

Who Are You?

One very important question to consider around "when" to retire is "How much is your identity tied up in what you do?" When you are good at your job and well-respected in your field, it is natural to think of yourself in terms of what you do: I am an editor; I am a therapist; I am a teacher; I am an engineer; etc. What would you say if someone asked you, "Who are you?" Can you separate your identity, your essential self, from your work? This seems particularly difficult for North Americans to do. We have found that in Europe, it is considered a bit rude to ask someone what they "do." People want to be seen in terms other than their work identity. But for most of us, it is difficult to separate the two. When we meet new people in North America, it's almost the first question we ask. Somehow, just saying "I'm retired" doesn't seem like enough.

Ron's step-father was a Los Angeles policeman. This was very much his identity and he was proud of it. When he hit mandatory retirement age, he was at a loss as to what to do with himself. He did not want to stop being a cop. His work had been his life. He had hobbies and was able to do any number of things but they were not central to his identity. After retirement, he lost motivation to do much of anything.

He started drinking heavily and within two years of retirement he died. For some people, whose work is their life, death comes even more quickly than this after they retire. These people might be better off gradually tapering off their work hours if possible and slowly getting accustomed to more free time.

On the other hand, Lois's father could not wait to retire. He was bored and unhappy in his government office work and retired as soon as he had his 30 years in. He was in his 50s and lived to be 91. He was glad to say that he had been retired more years than he had worked.

For those people who cannot wait to get away from jobs they hate, retirement looks like a relief for them. However, they could have problems with their new life if they have only focused on what they want to get away from and not on what they want to move toward. They may think of retirement as an endless long weekend, away from the pressures and unhappiness of their work. But retirement is not only about what you are leaving behind; it is also about what you are heading toward. If you have no vision of where you want to head, then retirement may be more difficult and you might struggle longer until you know what you want to do next.

For some people, retirement might mean leaving their employer, but continuing their work by being consultants in their field. Others meet their need for meaningful engagement in the world through volunteering. We live in Vancouver, which hosted the 2010 Winter Olympics. The Olympic organizing committee made use of 25,000 volunteers for this event, employed in all sorts of capacities, and the volunteers helped make it a successful event for everyone involved, including themselves. Most of the volunteers were retirees and they found the experience extremely rewarding.

So, if you think you are able to retire but don't know what you will do with yourself, maybe waiting would be wise, unless by doing the work in this book you develop a vision of

what you might do in retirement. If retirement only represents a loss of who you are and not a step toward who you
want to be, maybe you should hold off until you have that
vision.

How Do You Use Your Free Time?

We have discovered that many people who were reluctant to
retire enjoy their retired life much more than they expected.
They had no idea this would be the case. Their new life is
very satisfying, emotionally rewarding, and they do not miss
work at all. In addition, they are amazed to discover how
busy they become in retirement. It is nearly universal among
retirees to wonder, "How did I ever have time to work?"
When younger people who have not retired ask them, "What
do you do with all of your time?" they just laugh.

Very often people are hesitant to retire out of fear of the
unknown. Once they have done it, and have put some energy into figuring out what they want to do, they usually say,
"Why didn't I do this sooner?" Whether people have planned
or not, often unexpected opportunities arise for what they
can do. When they respond to the new possibilities, they discover talents or joys that surprise them.

One clue to whether you will enjoy yourself in retirement
is what you do with your free time while you are still working. If your weekends and holidays are still quite involved
with your work, and this is a matter of choice rather than
necessity, then you may have trouble being a retired person.
If you make use of your free time in a way that is totally different from your work life, then pay attention to that. It may
be a good pointer to what your vision for retirement might
be. While we were still working, we left town on weekends
and holidays and went off camping in places where we could
be active hiking, biking, kayaking, or skiing. It is no surprise
that much of our retired life consists of the same kind of
thing.

When to Start Your Planning for Life in Retirement

Most of you have probably been developing your dreams for retirement in a vague way for a long time, but may not have done much in a concrete way about fulfilling those dreams. Ideally, you will have started planning your life in retirement a year or more before you actually retire. Often it takes that long to get things lined up so you are ready to act when the time comes to quit working. This planning normally takes time to think through all of the issues and to discuss them with whoever else is involved. As a childless couple, we have been amazed at how many adult children of retiring couples object to their parents' retirement plans. It does not so much seem to be an issue of the parents spending their children's inheritance as it is the children wanting them to be more available for emotional support – not to mention babysitting. Each family has to sort out these issues in their own way.

Another factor that can affect retirement plans is your parents and their needs in old age. Our plans for retirement had to include options for some serious crisis or new living arrangements for our parents. We wanted to be available to them whenever they needed us. Retirement plans need to include the issues raised by being part of the sandwich generation, with both groups counting on you in some way. You need to spend some time thinking about when you will be available to these other two generations and when not, and for what sort of responsibilities.

It takes a certain amount of commitment to do an adequate planning job. Planning for enough money for retirement may be the easy part. Making plans for how you want to live in retirement may be more difficult. Many people are not that committed to doing planning for their lives and, of course, that is fine. Here is why we believe it is worth doing. We all tend to live within certain comfortable routines. When we do not plan, the daily routine takes over our lives and we end up not doing the things we often say we want to do. If we do not create space in our monthly and yearly calendar for these things to happen, then they do not happen. At least that is true for us. Thus, we make plans and put them in our calendar. Once they are in our calendar, we tend to do them.

The slogan of the American Association of Retired People (AARP) is "the power to make it better." Many people want to make their retirement years into something they really will be happy with; they want to make it better and they have the power to do so.

Some people actually over-plan for retirement. They pack in too many things and do not prioritize them. They do not build in enough leisure time for just enjoying the moment. They live their lives in just as busy a way as when they were working. We do not have to feel guilty about not working or not being busy. Rather than getting five things accomplished in a day, it is fine to accomplish only two, and to spend the rest of the day taking a nice walk, sitting and reading a book, hanging out with friends, or whatever.

People who become anxious about not having enough to do or having free, unstructured time in their lives when they do nothing may have to ease into retirement and gradually become comfortable with a more relaxed, laid-back lifestyle. To start with, they might have only one hour a day when they "do nothing." One of the main luxuries, we think, of retirement is having leisure time and doing the things that need doing in a more leisurely way. The ethic of hard work is now behind us. We have nothing to prove. We can relax and enjoy but, paradoxically, it may take some work and planning to make this happen.

Where to Live in Retirement

People tend to focus much of their planning energy on this big question. Entire books have been written on just this topic. Some people, like us, have travelled in different parts of the world and wondered, "What would it be like to live here?" We spent the first five years of our retirement addressing this question by living in different places and in different ways. This was part of our plan. Our modest, but paid-off house was quite rentable, and the rent we received helped us to fund our five moves during those years. We lived in small communities as well as living "on the road." We satisfied our wondering about what it would be like to live in the places we fantasized about. Ultimately, we sold our little house and settled in a 900-square-foot condo only five blocks away. We decided we really like the neighborhood we have lived in for so many years, and the condo is perfect for our life of frequent coming and goings.

This approach is clearly not for everyone. We encourage you, however, to be more open to different possibilities for deciding this question without rushing into anything. Consider various options and play with them. Living full-time in your vacation cottage may be tempting, but try it out first. Or try out a different community or different part of the country first by either renting for a while or doing a house exchange with other retirees. We recently did a five-month house exchange with a couple in southern England. This was our first, but their seventh. They love being able to live rent-free in different parts of the world, established in a real neighborhood.

One common issue about where to live is whether to downsize or not. This, of course, depends on how you plan to spend your time. If you want to focus more on your home and garden, the family home or an even larger house might be your choice. If travel is more important, a smaller more care-free place may work better. We encourage people to take their time with this question and not act immediately once they have retired.

Where you will live also depends on how you spend your free time now. If you go to concerts and plays and nice restaurants, a small town or rural community may not satisfy you no matter how much you have enjoyed vacations in that kind of place. If you mostly spend time at home with hobbies or activities around the house, staying in or moving to a small town may suit you fine.

We have ended up spending part of our winters in a retirement community in Arizona that offers both outdoor activities and city amenities. Having a second home was not in our original plan and only became part of our life after having visited there for winter vacations for a few years. But there are always places for sale in Arizona and Florida by people who moved there full-time and then decided it wasn't for them. So deciding where, in one way, comes last in the planning, after deciding when and what.

Chapter 3
Issues in Planning

*"We must always change, renew, rejuvenate ourselves;
otherwise we harden."*

GOETHE

Why Plan Your Retirement Life?

What will that first Monday after retirement look like? What will happen in that first week, or month, or year? Where will you live and what will "home" be like? Will you have the kind of relationships you want? If you have a partner, will you have made some agreement with him or her about how much time you will be together or apart? Will there be any shift in household responsibilities? Will you be living a life that incorporates principles of healthy aging? Will you continue with some form of work? What sort of leisure activities will you have? Will you have some goals you want to pursue or some passion that will absorb you? What is going to bring you the most pleasure or feel most rewarding? Will your retired life be everything you have hoped it would be? Generally, unless you plan differently, whatever routine you establish at the beginning of this new phase of life will be what you do for the rest of your retirement.

Whether you can answer these questions and whether you have a clear sense of what your retirement will be like depends on the planning you do. Retirement is your opportunity to put together the life you most want to live, but it may take some work to figure out what that life is. One approach to retirement could be as simple as a T-shirt we saw in a ski resort town: "Quit work, get some stuff, go somewhere, have fun." That is a kind of a plan. It probably does not take much time to figure out, at least if you are a young person taking a year or two off from pursuing more adult challenges. Retirement is the best opportunity we will ever have for deciding what we do "when we grow up."

One friend of ours says, "I don't plan. I just do stuff." In his case, much of what he does is a scaled-down version of what he had been doing in his work life and it remains interesting to him. His former work life provides the structure for much of his retired life except for not showing up at an office 9 to 5. He has less stress and fills in the time between work projects with more unplanned leisure activities. He has never taken much time to think about the question, "What do I most want to do with my life now?"

In one survey, 50% of retired people said that they had not spent enough time thinking about their life in retirement. In another survey, 70% of retiring people said they had made no plans for this new phase of life. In our own case, we knew that if we entered retirement with no plan, we would not do many of the things we had said over the years that we wanted to do when we had the time.

Whether or not your life in retirement becomes everything you want it to be depends only on you and what you do to bring it about. You may even have some image of what "the good life" will be for you, but if you have not done the concrete planning needed to achieve it, it likely will not happen. It would be too bad to have spent years putting away money for your retirement, planning your financial goals and executing those plans, and then not know what to do with the time you have when the day arrives.

One person called planning a kind of "mental time travel, roaming around in the future." We think of it as a more concrete activity than that, but the image is useful. Another man said to us, "All I know is that I don't want to retire the way my father did." He was clear about what he did not want. He had a negative plan. Unfortunately, that is usually not enough.

Some people approach retirement with the famous "bucket list" in hand. Lois gave Ron a daily tear-off calendar called 1000 Places to See Before You Die. He saves the ones he would like to see and they might become a part of a plan. Having a list of places to see and things to do is an ongoing part of our planning, but there is more to planning life in retirement than this. The list can be a part of it, but it does not represent, in our way of thinking, an adequate job of planning.

Planning and Spontaneity

Anyone who has been in business at the corporate level is familiar with planning, especially long-range and strategic planning. The plan helps a company to think about their direction in business, how to get there, and what to do about the threats and opportunities they foresee. The plan helps keep them focused on their "mission," without being distracted by less important issues. The same goes for a life in retirement plan.

Having a plan for your life does not mean that everything is written in stone and must be done. We have planned for things that we later lost energy for and realized we did not really want to do. We all have the freedom to change our plans. However, for the most part, planning opens up new avenues and breaks us out of old patterns.

Even within a plan, it is possible and often desirable to live spontaneously. We need to be open to great, unexpected opportunities that come along. For example, Lois never wanted anything to do with whitewater rafting. It was not on our list. Then, friends took a trip down the Colorado River through the Grand Canyon, raved about it and we said, "Let's try it." It was wonderful. At another point, Lois had the chance to work as an extra in movies being made in Vancouver. She had never conceived of such a thing, but gave it a whirl and had a lot of fun with it. Other things have happened like this, and we fit them into the plan. We are always open to spontaneous opportunities.

Having a basic plan helps us to evaluate the opportunities that come along and decide whether to pursue them or not. One of the challenges of retirement for us has been the abundant opportunities we have had to do things. There are so many attractive options for how we could spend our time. We can check each opportunity against our plan and ask, "Does this fit with what we know about ourselves and how we want to live our life?" Our planning has helped us say no to things that were "opportunities," but did not really fit with our overall goals for life. Ron still does the occasional workshop for people related to his professional field and his writing. But he does not accept all invitations. They have to fit in with our plan and goals. On the other hand, having a plan based on traveling did not stop us from tying ourselves down to a winter home in Tucson, which did in fact fit with our overall goals, though in a way we had not foreseen.

Planning and Emotion

Planning for retirement takes intentionality and self-discipline. If we simply "go with our feelings" then we could end up directionless since feelings change with circumstances. That is like sailing only where the wind takes you, which is fine if that satisfies you. However, too many people use feelings as their guide to making life decisions and do not exercise thoughtful foresight. Feelings are only one component of decision-making. Making a serious life decision according to the feelings of the moment can lead to serious regrets later on.

Depressed people are often advised to exercise more and to socialize more. They say in response, "I don't feel like it." They do not do it and their depression does not lift. There is plenty of research that says our feelings will change if we first change our behavior or the environment. Feelings exist in response to particular circumstances. Change the circumstance and the feelings will change.

Remember Joseph Campbell's advice to "follow your bliss"? Pay attention to what makes you passionate about life. Do not censor yourself. At this point in life, you are allowed to aim for what you want to do. Look at what really turns you on. If your plans are not invested with your deepest wishes and wants, they most likely will not happen. Your heart will not be in it. If you have passion for your plans, this will make it worth the extra work the plans may require.

If your plans evoke too much anxiety, you will not pursue them no matter how passionate you feel about them. The anxiety will undercut the plan. There are two ways to approach this anxiety. Either work on reducing it or respect it and give up on any plans that evoke hyper-anxiety. Any personal growth or change is likely to create some degree of anxiety, but you can draw upon previous experiences to challenge your uneasiness. Ask, "What have I learned about myself and my anxiety over the years? How have I managed it in the past?" What are some examples where you have been decisive, faced the anxiety, taken the risk, and acted? What are examples where you failed to do so?

Some people are uncomfortable with decision-making in general. They do not like the responsibility of deciding and then committing to doing a certain thing. "What if it doesn't go well and I fail?" The fearful feeling keeps them from acting. Lois can occasionally experience this paralysis. She challenges it by saying to herself, "What's the worst that could happen?" Dealing with this question tends to get her moving.

Related to the skill of foresight is that of being able to delay gratification, to be able to put off getting a good feeling now so that it will feel much better in the future. People who have been successful in their lives have usually done this. Those who are unhappy with their lives are often unable to delay gratification; they have typically gone with their feelings at the time in making their decisions. They do not ask, "Where does doing this thing that feels good now take me in terms of my life goals?"

Making good plans also requires being honest with yourself about who you are and what you truly want out of life.

Delaying gratification does not mean never being gratified. Making plans based on what you think you "should" do is just as unrealistic. "Should" plans are usually quickly abandoned. Our energy usually goes to the things we want to do.

The questions in this book ask you to think as well as feel. We ask you to think first about your life up to the present time and then, based on what you learn about yourself, how you want your future life to go. We ask you to think about your life goals. This is essential to doing good planning for your life in retirement. It takes a certain amount of emotional maturity to not only make plans but, more importantly, to carry them out.

Planning As a Couple

This book assumes you are working with a partner who will be part of your retired life. If you live alone, you can also use this book, but we encourage you to discuss the exercises with someone close to you. Talking aloud about your responses helps you to test the honesty and reality of what you have written.

It is normal for partners to have quite different visions of and expectations for retirement. In a TD Waterhouse survey of retired couples, only half of them said the two partners had the same vision of retirement. A couple may have done a certain amount of planning for their future over the course of a relationship, but few talk seriously about their life together in retirement.

Ron has worked with couples who discovered only after retirement that they had quite different visions of what their life would be like. When one partner wants to stay home, work on their hobbies, or be closely involved with grandchildren and the other wants to travel the world, they are both in for a nasty surprise. While planning may not bring them eye to eye, they will at least see they have some work to do to develop a life in retirement that is satisfying for both of them.

Before retiring, most couples have established a pattern for how they live their daily lives. They have divided their household functioning in a particular way that worked for them at the time. They have built-in time apart, related to their jobs, where they ran their own lives themselves and did not have to consult with their partner about their decisions. Upon retiring, they start bumping into each other in the house. Their routines are disrupted. Each may think the other is impinging on their space and on their lives. Before Ron retired, Lois told him the saying, "Retirement means half the money and twice the husband." He thought this was a compliment! It took him a while to realize that maybe she was not thrilled by the prospect of him being around all the time. As many wives have said, "I married you for better or for worse, but not for lunch."

PART II
Working on Retirement
(Exercises)

Chapter 4
Where Have You Been?

"Your job today tells me nothing about your future – your use of your leisure today tells me just what your tomorrow will be."

ROBERT H. JACKSON

Looking Back before Looking Forward

In order to create a happier life in your future, it helps to look back at how you have achieved happiness in the past. The past is the foundation we have created for the future life we want to build. This chapter provides an opportunity to do a review of your life, from as far back as you can remember up to the present. Good planning for the future partly depends on what you have done and how you understand your past. Moving into the future, you want to maintain what has been good in your life and avoid making the same mistakes.

Your past life becomes a kind of automatic guidance system that encompasses your:

- beliefs and values,
- goals and principles,
- anxieties and fears,
- desires and wishes,
- and actions in work and relationships.

This chapter will help you be clearer about the trajectory of your life and decide whether you are happy with it or not.

In looking at the reality of who you have been and how you have managed your life up to the present, you can be more realistic about the kind of life you want to create in the future.

The exercises that follow will be somewhat repetitious. The intent is for you to revisit the same experiences from different angles or perspectives. As a result of doing these exercises, you can decide if you are happy with the direction your life is taking and want to maintain it or do a course correction or a total change of direction. Retirement gives us the opportunity to do any of this.

How to Do These Exercises

See Chapter 8 for a link to download these exercises. The exercises are a series of questions with no "correct" answers. You can write out your answers or just think them. We strongly suggest that you write your answers. Putting it in writing helps to focus your thoughts, to take the planning more seriously, and to make changes as you read through your answers. It is also helpful and fun to go back in a few years and look at what you wrote to see if you are fulfilling your stated goals and plans, whether things need to be revisited, or whether whole new, unanticipated areas have emerged that might call for a new plan.

Any plan you make is not meant to be static in any case. You need to be open to having a plan that is constantly evolving and responding to outside events in your life or to new insights. Being flexible and adaptable within a plan is almost as important as making the plan.

The exercises in this chapter will take time to complete. One can do them on a piecemeal basis, over a period of weeks, grabbing an evening here or there. We recommend, however, that you set aside a large block of time, like a long weekend, and dedicate most of that time to doing the exercises. They can be completed within a leisurely two and one-half to three days. When we do them, we like to hole up a hotel in some nice setting, not have to worry about cooking, or doing chores, or being distracted by work or phone calls, and just focus on doing the exercises. We build in breaks for a walk or something relaxing.

The exercises in Chapters 5 and 6 can be done in an evening each, and then those in Chapter 7, focusing on the future, may require another weekend. You can make photocopies of all the workbook pages so you each have your own to write on.

Exercise 1
Life Review

1. Take a clean sheet of paper and turn it on its side. Write Birth on the left side and Present on the right.

   Draw a line from left to right, representing your life from your birth up to the present. As you move across the page, move the line up or down to indicate periods of satisfaction and happiness in your life or unhappiness – the low points in life. Do not think about this exercise too much.

2. Break this line into specific periods in your life: infancy, childhood, adolescence (through high school), young adulthood, mature adulthood, and later adulthood up to the present. You might depict these periods with vertical lines that mark a temporal separation or transition between them.

3. Indicate on the line significant dates that relate to the highs and lows, turning points, or important events and make a brief note about each one.

4. Show your sheet to your partner and talk about what this line means to you and why you have drawn it as you have. Take turns listening to each other talk about your life stories. Do not make evaluative (positive or negative) comments about the other's story. Instead, do your best

to ask information questions that will help your partner think further about why he or she has drawn the line in this way.

5. If you have not already done so, discuss the major turning points in your life and what made them so important.

6. If you have not already done this as a part of telling your story, discuss what relationships were significant for you (in a positive or negative way) at each period of life. How did these relationships affect your life and the major turning points?

Take as much time as you want to discuss this life-line with your partner. There is no reason to rush this exercise. Of course, as with any of the exercises that follow, you can return to discuss it again later when you have, no doubt, had more thoughts about it.

Exercise 2

1. Summarize in writing what you have understood about yourself and your life in this first life review exercise. Do this in one or two paragraphs at the most.

2. Read aloud and then discuss what you have written with your partner.

Exercise 3

1. In no more than one paragraph or a short list for each one, write down your response to each of these questions:

    a. What has provided meaning in your life? This question is not necessarily some heavy philosophical or religious question – you can go there if you want – but more about what has motivated you all along and got you moving in life. Has there been a driving force or a theme that runs through your life?

b. Are you happy with this view of your life? Is there some "meaning" or motivation you are still looking for or want to discover?

c. What have you most valued in your life? What has been important to you that you want always to have as a part of your life as you look into the future? What would you just as soon do without?

d. What principles have you lived by over the years at various stages of life that have guided your decision-making? These could be consciously held principles that you very clearly chose for yourself or ones that you were not aware of until now.

e. What goals have you had, at each stage of your life? To what extent have they been fulfilled?

f. What has your work meant to you throughout your life? (Note: "work" includes being a homemaker.)

g. Besides remuneration, what has your work given you? How has it benefitted you?

h. Overall, how happy have you been with your work life? What are you thinking of when you answer this question?

i. What regrets, if any, do you have about your life in general?

j. Do you have any sense of how you could make up for these regrets, if at all, in the way you live your life in the future?

2. Read your responses aloud, point by point, and discuss each one of these questions with your partner.

3. What has emerged for you out of this exercise and discussion? Write it down on a separate piece of paper, with a heading of "My Life So Far." Include something about what has been most and least satisfying in your life and what was going on to create this experience.

This is an opportunity to make some generalizations about your life based on your specific, individual experiences.

Exercise 4

1. Divide a clean sheet of paper down the middle with a line. On the left-hand side write down all the jobs you have had in your life (starting with your jobs as a kid), and all of the positions you have held. If you have never worked outside of the home, break down the various jobs at different stages you have done as a homemaker. On the right-hand side, next to each job or position, write brief answers to the following questions:

   ♦ How good or how competent were you at doing this job?

   ♦ What were the specific things you liked and disliked about this job?

   ♦ What, if anything, would you like to have done differently in this job?

2. Show your sheet of jobs to your partner and then explain your responses.

3. Discuss the specific things in these jobs you will be sad or glad to leave behind.

4. Discuss in general what satisfactions and dissatisfactions you have had in your work life.

Exercise 5

1. Write down all of the most memorable holidays (vacations) you have had in your life. Go back as far as childhood if you wish. Where did you go and what did you do that made it memorable? Are there any experiences that you want to be sure never to repeat again because you did not enjoy them? What did you have to do to make

it a good experience? Are any of the good experiences things that you want to build into your future life in retirement?

2. Read aloud and then discuss what you wrote with your partner.

Exercise 6

1. Write down all the leisure activities you do now. This could be everything from knitting to hang-gliding, gardening to concert-going.

2. Now rank them according to the most important to keep doing or do more of.

Exercise 7

1. Write a two-page biography of your life up to this point using the suggested questions below.

   ◆ Other than giving places and events or experiences, try to address the question "Who am I?" in each time period. What words or phrases come to mind?

   ◆ Where have you found meaning in your life and how has that been expressed on a daily basis?

   ◆ What values and personal character strengths have you attempted to uphold in your life and how well have you done? Do you have some specific examples in mind?

   ◆ Characterize what has given you the greatest satisfaction in your life — the most enjoyment and happiness. Include things that you might call your "peak experiences." What made them peak experiences?

   ◆ What have been the disappointing parts of your life? What was your part in making them so? What do you need to do to avoid these in the future?

- Include the things that were/are going on in your personal life and your life in relationships that you want to maintain no matter what else happens in your life.

- Include the nature and quality of your relationships with important people in your life over time.

2. Read aloud and then discuss what you have written with your partner.

Exercise 8

Discuss with your partner your thoughts in response to each group of words or phrases below. We mean them to be somewhat general and vague so that you can go wherever your mind carries you. Include how much or how little you want each one in your life, what you think you might have to do to achieve them or realize them, and what you want to avoid.

- health, physical abilities, personal appearance

- sense of security, where I live

- adventure, recreation, relaxation, leisure

- fulfilling roles or experiences, responsibilities, sense of identity, employment

- level of wealth, material possessions, transportation wants or needs

- satisfying love life, sexuality, sensuality and sensual wishes, comfort

- giving and receiving affection, effective communication, close relationships

- togetherness, separateness, autonomy in living, home and family life

- friendships, having the respect of others, and giving respect

- religious/spiritual life, meaning and purpose, aesthetic wishes

- serving others

- being an informed citizen, involvement in local or national politics

- anything else that you want to include in this list.

Exercise 9

Write out, then read aloud and discuss with your partner what the word or the idea of "retirement" means to you at this moment after doing this life review.

Chapter 5

The Transition into Retirement

"If you can spend a perfectly useless afternoon in a perfectly useless manner, you have learned how to live."

LIN YUTANG

The questions in this chapter are a guide to thinking about what retirement means to you. After you have read the questions and made notes about your answers, you and your partner can discuss them in an evening. If you are already retired, try to transpose the questions so that they apply to your life in retirement.

1. How anxious do you think you will be when retirement happens?

2. What do you think your anxiety is about?

Apart from financial concerns, what else might stimulate anxiety in you about retiring? Remembering that anxiety represents some kind of threat (real or imagined), what could possibly be threatening in retirement? For example, how might your sense of well-being be affected, or your sense of identity, or your connections with others? Some people worry that whoever replaces them at work will do a better job, or they will not be missed, or the new person will be more popular. Others worry that the new friends they make in their retirement life will not have any sense of how important they were in their work setting or how much it meant to them.

3. How difficult do you think it will be to "let go" of your workplace?

Some people find it easy to walk away from their office, and others find it very difficult. Any number of factors may enter into this and it is not always easy to predict. People who thought it would be easy have been amazed at how much they miss it, and vice versa.

4. What in particular might be hard to let go of, and is there any way to build this thing into your retirement?

There will be losses as you transition to a new life. What will they be for you? How big a deal will this be? What adjustments do you expect to have to make? What things will you be sad to lose? Did you enjoy going into your workplace? Do you expect to make a clean break from work or will it be a slow, lingering departure with some kind of regular, ongoing contact with your work, but at a reduced level?

5. What work issues will you be escaping from or trying to avoid in the future?

What will you be happy to stop doing and "can't wait till it is over"?

6. What does retirement mean to you now, in this context, as you think about it?

Does the word retirement have negative connotations for you? Does it mean to you that you are "over the hill," "being put out to pasture," or "being dumped for new blood"? Is it more like "getting out of jail" or "flying free"? Or what? How did you think of retirement when you were much younger? Do you still think of it that way now? How did other people in your life refer to retirement and how did that affect your views of it?

7. Did you see close family members retire and how did they do it?

If you observed your parents or other older people retire, did the way they do it have any impact on you? Have you ever spoken with any of these people about their experience of retiring? If you know people who have retired, could you talk with them about what it has been like for them? If you have spoken with people about it, what sort of thoughts or attitudes did you pick up from them?

8. To what extent were you in charge of your own schedule in your workplace?

People whose work required them to plan their workday and the jobs they did are probably going to be more at ease planning their retirement. Those who were simply told what to do each day, and did only that, may have more difficultly working out a schedule for themselves. Part of the freedom of retirement is planning how we use our time, but not everyone has experience doing this. Some people might be anxious about how to fill the time.

9. On balance, would you say that retirement for you is more about "getting away" from something or more about "moving toward" something?

Any way you look at it, retirement is a kind of a loss. It may be a happy or sad loss, but the fact that something that structured so much of your time is now removed from your life means it is a loss. Those who replace the loss with something they are eagerly looking forward to will generally find retirement to be an easier and happier experience.

10. To what extent would you say that your work is central to your identity?

When you introduce yourself to others, how central is your work in how you want to be known to them? Is it front and center in your mind or is there something else you want people to know about you? We mentioned Ron's stepfather earlier, whose work as a policeman was so central to who he was that mandatory retirement became a kind of death knell for him. In spite of being an intelligent man, he had nothing to replace that life with and did not recover from the loss.

Most people have never thought much about the question of who they are apart from their work, whether it is in a career, or as a parent, or homemaker. If there had never been a job in your life, or even a family, how would you go about defining your life? What images of life would you have if you had never worked, or married, or had a family of your own?

One image of life without work that we like is the ancient Greek idea of simply being a "citizen." The Greek aristocracy, much like the English aristocracy of the 18th and 19th centuries, viewed work as demeaning and thought that being an active and responsible citizen of their community was their highest calling. This image works for us without, of course, all of the implications of being part of an aristocracy.

11. What is the experience of aging like for you? How well do you think you will age?

We speak of people who age gracefully. Whatever it means, it does seem to be a kind of ideal. Neither of us has particularly welcomed the experience of aging. For Ron, his identity has been more invested in his physical abilities than in his work life. He was always active, physically competent, and coordinated. It has been hard for him to accept that there are many physical things that he can no longer do or do the way he did as a younger, stronger person. He has no choice but to accept what is happening and he has had to work on his attitude toward it in order to age more gracefully.

With a failing memory, there are things that we knew so well and thought we would never forget that just disappear. Ron has over 7000 of our travel photos on his laptop screen saver. The random photos remind him of things he had long forgotten. Sometimes he will just sit and watch one picture after another come up, which stimulates old memories of experiences he has loved. He told Lois that if he gets to the stage of being confined to bed, to just put his laptop in front of him playing these pictures and he will be content.

As we age, we learn more and more to say "goodbye." Sometimes we do it with thanks, or regret, or deep sorrow, or with a sense of hope of what is to come since there could be new places and people (even new loves), and fun activities to discover along with the leave-taking. We also say goodbye to our own face and body that we lived with so long. It may not have been great, but at least it was young. Living a pain-free life is something else we say goodbye to. Sometimes, most every day, something hurts physically and makes us aware that our body is failing us.

12. What do you know about your own coping skills as you deal with change?

What major changes in life have you had to deal with in the past? How well did you manage with them? What coping skills did you draw on? How might you need to strengthen your coping skills? Some people become more anxious when dealing with major changes and become reactive. They snap at others or blame others for having to make the changes in their life that are in fact quite reasonable to make, but which they resist.

Conclusion

As we indicated at the beginning of this chapter, we mean this chapter to be thought-provoking. No one can predict exactly what moving into retirement will be like, but this is a chance to explore what it *might* be like for you.

Chapter 6

General Issues for a Happy Retired Life

"Retirement – that happy age when a man can be idle with impunity."

WASHINGTON IRVING

An Attitude of Gratitude

Not everyone who retires moves toward a happier life. For some, retirement means trying to live on a much reduced income and barely scraping by if at all. Many of those at poverty level in North America are the elderly despite having worked hard all of their life. They have to rely on friends and family or social welfare programs and perhaps make use of food banks and similar resources. They were never able to make enough to live on when they worked and have even less income when retired. Those who have stopped work usually did not just "retire," they simply could not go to work anymore because of medical problems and physical disabilities resulting from those problems that they could not afford to take care of when they were younger.

The paragraph above probably does not describe most of you who are reading this book. Planning your life in retirement is a luxury that most of the world does not enjoy. You are likely fortunate enough to have accumulated a certain amount of money and have had access to some decent medical care. In one study after another, a primary indicator of those who are happy and healthy in their later years is a grateful attitude. This is not simply about the financial capital we have managed to accumulate and live on. It includes the relationships we have enjoyed and nurtured over the years that have become a part of who we are. Indeed, these rate more highly on people's scales of importance than does the amount of money they have in the bank. Very rich but lonely people who lack close relationships do not usually do well in their retirement years.

Gratitude includes a sense of humility. If we have an attitude of "look at everything I have accomplished. What a great job I have done. It has all been my doing and no one else contributed anything to what I have achieved," then the sense of gratitude will be absent. This stance ignores what has been given to us early in life. We are indebted to family, mentors, and others who have shown us how to live or given us a chance; to partners and friends who have supported us along the way; to coworkers who have each contributed in their own ways; and to countless numbers of people we have never met – most of them much poorer than us – who have supported our particular work and in ways we will never fully understand.

There is no question that we have made good and sometimes fortuitous decisions in our life and worked hard to pursue our goals. That is our own doing. And yet, we cannot ignore all that has been given to us through these other means and through the larger networks that we have been a part of. They are significant contributors to our health and happiness. Author Malcolm Gladwell's book *Outliers: The Story of Success* shows just how this has worked in the lives of some of the well-known and highly successful people he writes about.

Money Does Count in the Happiness Equation, But ...

However, a happy retired life always has to have a hedge against the unfortunate losses and economic disasters that can occur. Certainly having relatively safe reserve funds in the bank for unanticipated emergencies is a part of this. However, as we've said, this book is not about the financial aspects of retirement. Many other issues beyond finances are related to a happy retirement and need to be a part of everyone's plans for retirement. They represent the equivalent of a sizeable emotional bank account that will help support us well into old age. Central to these issues is our physical, emotional, and psychological health.

In this chapter, we focus on a few basic issues that you need to plan for to have a happy retirement. We expect that you will have an ongoing focus on these issues both in preparation for retirement and throughout your remaining years. Following are questions that you need to consider individually if you live alone or to discuss with a partner. In most cases, such as where to retire as a couple, the questions are not simply a matter of individual preference. Both people need to agree on and support the plans.

As with the previous chapter, read over the numbered questions and the notes following, make notes, and then discuss your thoughts with your partner.

1. What are you doing to maintain good physical health for the coming years?

It is obvious that without your health, little else can matter for having a happy retirement. "The first wealth is health." It is critical that you spend time thinking about what will develop and support a healthy life.

Exercise and diet are central features of a physically healthy life. A great deal has been written on the need for strength training and aerobic exercise for older people. How will you incorporate these into your retired life?

Older people also need to pay attention to the dangers of the metabolic syndrome — the five inter-related health issues of diabetes, obesity, high blood pressure, stroke, and heart disease. Each one can be debilitating and interfere with a happy retirement. The good news is that these medical issues are very responsive to changes in exercise and diet and are preventable.

The bad news is that there is disagreement even among scientists and doctors about what a good diet is. In the 20th century, the pendulum swung from starches are bad to fat is bad, to some fat is bad, to carbohydrates are bad, to some carbohydrates are bad. Funding issues and politics have made a shambles of the research efforts, so contradictory reports appear every year.

The most objective and scientific book we have seen that looks at the issue is *Good Calories, Bad Calories* by science journalist Gary Taubes. You might also look at *The End of Illness* by David B. Agus. We encourage you to look into the health issue more deeply than the latest newspaper article.

Age and illness are not synonymous terms. We do not want to reach a later point in life and say, as so many have, "If I'd known I was going to live so long, I would have taken better care of myself." Count on it, you will probably live longer than you once expected and the quality of that life depends on how well you take care of your health.

If you have not done so, we encourage you to get a medical assessment of your present physical health and decide on what you need to do to improve.

2. What are you doing to maintain good psychological health?

Emotional maturity and psychological health are also important for a good and happy retirement. Unhappy and upsetting feelings can be just as damaging as specific physical complaints that go unattended. If you are lonely, or full of anger, or dominated by debilitating anxiety and fears, or depressed, then attention needs to be paid. All of these can be addressed and improved.

Counseling has been shown to be as good as medication for many conditions, without the side effects. For example, depression, at various levels of intensity, is a major factor in our society with some studies saying that up to 50% of people over 45 suffer from its effects. Counseling helps significantly with this condition.

Traditionally, the various psychological disciplines have focused on emotional disabilities and mental disease. In recent years, the growing field of "positive psychology" has focused more on developing the skills to improve our emotional well-being and level of happiness.

Specific to the issue of retirement, positive psychology says that how we think about aging affects the quality of our lives and the degree of happiness we will feel. There is a bit of self-fulfilling prophesy involved here. If I think it will be awful, it will be. If I think it will be wonderful, it will be. According to the research on happiness, this is true no matter what the reality of the situation is. Two people can break a leg and have a completely different reaction to it.

One major skill of emotionally healthy and mature people is flexibility. No matter how well we plan, life will intervene and the unexpected roadblock will crop up. The rigid person will just be stopped by it, but the flexible person will adapt and figure out a different way to go, even look at it as an opportunity to explore new territory.

To learn more about psychological well-being, look into courses in your community or read *Seven Strategies for Positive Aging* by Robert D. Hill or *Aging Well* by George E. Vaillant. In summarizing his book, Vaillant lists seven factors that the people who aged well in his extensive longitudinal studies had in common:

1. not being a smoker;

2. adaptive coping style;

3. absence of alcohol abuse;

4. healthy weight;

5. stable marriage;

6. exercise;

7. many years of education.

People who had these qualities (or at least 5 or 6 of them) at age 50 were the most likely to age well as they grew older.

Part of psychological health involves having an interest in, even a passion for, something outside yourself. Retirement provides an opportunity to renew old interests as well as to explore new ones. One could return to old skills long neglected or develop new ones. What is it that will keep your inner self alive and involved? One friend, when he retired, was able to return to a passion he had as a young man. He loved old radios. He established an internet business to seek out and repair very old radios and then sell them on Ebay. It gave him joy to do this, and he established new friends in far away places.

Retirement is when you can focus on new kinds of creativity. There is time now to devote to painting or photography. One friend was told as a child that she was tone deaf and could not sing. Now, in retirement, she has been taking voice lessons and has discovered that she can sing and is thoroughly enjoying it. Two friends have taken up square dancing, which requires developing physical skills as well as mental in learning all of the steps.

In addition, you may have skills to teach to others. Contact the various educational resources in your community about giving a class in your particular area of interest and ability. You might be surprised at how much they would welcome you teaching a course on a topic that you know something about.

Those who live with some sort of chronic and debilitating disease can move in the direction of greater emotional well-being and creativity. In an AARP magazine article, Richard M. Cohen, an Emmy award-winning TV producer who has a challenging chronic disease, says, "To live well with a chronic illness is largely a mind game.... Think about who you are and how you want to live. How will you make the most out of your life now? Do not stifle your dreams." The Paralympic Games show us people who have decided to live well with their disabilities.

The magazine article goes on to point out that in 2009, there were at least 133 million people in the United States living with chronic disease. Those who are willing to be more active in managing their disease can save money and improve their quality of life. Disease self-management programs can help you achieve your goals for living with chronic illness. *Living a Healthy Life with Chronic Conditions* by Kate Lorig is worth reading.

3. What are you doing to improve or maintain relationships with family and friends?

Plenty of research shows that physical and emotional health is tied in closely with the quality of the relationships people have with their parents, other relatives, and their friends. For example, studies have shown that those who have a good marriage at age 50 have a better chance of living well at age 80. Surprising to some, this is a better indicator of a good old age than the level of cholesterol at age 50.

Extended family is also important. For example, every parent has to decide what kind of support or help, if any, they will give their adult children and grandchildren and how much they will be involved with them in their retirement years. Normally, patterns in this area have been long established by the time retirement comes along. Now is a time to redo these patterns if you are not happy with them. Ron's book *Family Ties That Bind* is a guide to looking at and dealing with the family issues that are a part of our life.

Some retirees make a point of moving closer to where their children and grandchildren live, and others make a point of putting some distance between them. The physical closeness or distance is not the essential thing. Generally, in this time of greater instability, it is somewhat risky to choose your retirement residence on the basis of "being close to the kids and grandkids." They could take new jobs in other communities or split the family into different locations through divorce. Cell phones and internet options like Skype can provide immediate access to family wherever they are.

We find it sad when retired people have been and remain cut off from their own family of origin. A good retirement project, if one has not already done it, is to slowly work on improving all of your family relationships. If your parents are still alive and you have been distant from them, it will make the process of dealing with their decline and deaths much better if you can improve your connection with them now.

Good relationships rarely result when the parents are over-involved with their adult children and keep giving them advice, whether asked for or not. They have their own independent lives, but you can still be friends and hear about their lives. It is not helpful to them if you are bailing them out of trouble all of the time.

One area that tends to be difficult is the in-law relationship. Parents often blame their son/daughter-in-law for problems that their own child also participates in. Getting along with a son or daughter- in-law is essential. Remember, that growing up in a different family, they will have their own ways of doing things (e.g., parenting), and it is not your job to tell them "how we do it in our family." It will be good for everyone in the family, including yourself, if you find a way to be both connected and emotionally separate from them.

Of course, your close friendships with non-family members will be well established if you choose to retire where you have always lived. However, just as with adult children, staying in that area only because of your friends being there is risky. Many of them will move away when they retire. You cannot count on them being there in your old age.

If you move to a retirement community, where people have moved from other parts of the country, you will find it is easy to make friends. Everyone is in the same boat. They do not usually have a huge number of well-established, long-term friends and generally welcome getting to know new people. On the other hand, if you move to a long-established, stable community that has been unchanged for many years, it may be difficult to break into any friendship groups.

4. What do you think about the purpose of life, and how you will pursue yours?

Most people have already given some thought to this question and have begun to invest themselves in their own sense of purpose. If you have not, retirement is the perfect time to revisit this question. Even if you believe with Camus that there is no given or prescribed purpose to life, then it is your job (he says) to create it. Do you have a faith or a spiritual tradition that you practice? Do you want to do anything more with it or explore it further?

Related to this issue is the question of altruism. This quality is closely related to the ability to have a good, healthy, and meaningful life. In what ways do you already, or would you like to, give to others? How can you make the lives of others better? If you have been blessed with significant material advantages, how will you pass them on?

As mentioned, research on emotionally healthy people indicates that they have a strong ability to practice gratitude. Their thankfulness for what they have received is translated into giving to others in some way. A warm giving of self to others can be a way of distracting ourselves from our own difficulties. It can be an antidote to a sense of bitterness for what we never had. Rather than being continuously unhappy about never getting it, we can find a wonderful resolution to these feelings by giving that quality to others.

Volunteering is a common retirement activity. What types of service opportunities are available where you live? How much time do you want to give to it? There are many kinds of opportunities for making a contribution to the quality of life of others. Search them out. Many times, this kind of caring does not have to be a formal "job," but simply making an extra effort with people you know who are lonely or need help with getting out. One friend of ours has made it his project to visit or take out elderly people in his church (more elderly than he is!). Although he does it as a "duty," it is rewarding for him as well.

5. What are your thoughts about and how are you preparing for really old age?

We need to be looking further down the road than just this immediate, enjoyable start of retirement. Although this is a new beginning, there is indeed an end to it all. Our planning needs to take that into account. Most likely, you have already had or will soon have a rehearsal for dying as your own parents or other family members go through the experience. What can you learn from this?

Adult children who are trying to help their aged parents often find the parents to be "stubborn" and unwilling to seek out the resources that are available to help them with the challenges of old age. Lois's 91-year-old father became much less stable when he walked, but he would not use a cane or a walker. He found it demeaning. Only after he fell a couple of times (luckily not breaking any bones) did he agree to using a walker and then he said, "Hey, I can get around much easier with this thing."

The question experiences like this with our parents raises is, "Will I be like that when I get really old? Will my kids have the same frustration with me that I have with my parents?" Now is a good time to think about how we want to grow into really old age, and what kinds of resources we will want to draw on. We may all say, "I'll never be in that condition," but we can't control it. If we avoid planning for the worst, we both abandon the opportunity to be more in charge of this process and put the responsibility for these decisions on our children or other relatives who may not take kindly to it or, do it as we would wish.

As you watch your own parents and family members cope with extreme old age, what are you learning about your attitudes to death and dying? Ron never thought much about this question until his mother became fatally ill. After many years of being distant from her, he was able to get much closer to her and then be around as she moved toward death. He was grateful for the opportunity. They talked about how she was handling the experience, and he learned a great deal from it. In a very real sense, with Ron's support, she was in charge of her dying, and slowly shed her material possessions along the way. When she died, Ron carried one bag of clothing out of the nursing home and that was all he had to deal with. She had already distributed her belongings on her own.

Unlike his mother, Ron's aunt died in old age having done nothing to prepare for the inevitable. She left behind a two-story house with a basement and attic full of a life-time of collected effects. Ron, the only remaining relative, had no idea who she wanted her various things to go to and ended up just giving stuff to charities. It felt sad to deal with her life of memories in this way. If she had been more in charge of the dying process, rather than ignoring the reality of what was coming, she could have made her own decisions and made the end easier for Ron.

How do you see yourself when you are really old? When you have lost the physical or mental powers to fully take care of yourself? How will you prepare for it? Have you spoken with your children or friends or whoever will be involved about what you expect and how you would like things to proceed? Do you want a Living Will and, if so, what have you done about it? What might you put in writing in general about what decisions you expect to be made on your behalf? What sort of legacies do you want to leave after your death?

Wills can be tricky issues for families after the death of a parent. Not infrequently, Ron encountered in his counseling practice a family whose dead parent's will contained surprises that threw them into chaos. It was clear the parent was trying to address some old grievance or sense of emotional imbalance in the family that had not been talked about before. It was a disservice to the family members not to have addressed the issues that the will revealed. It removed the opportunity to work through the unresolved issues in a more satisfactory way while the parent was still alive.

Will your will surprise your family members? How might you address now the issues you are trying to rectify in your will so that everyone has had a chance to hear your thoughts and discuss them? What needs to be said now to the people involved so that the reasons for your decision are clear to all involved? Ron's mother did this with all of the people involved in her family. She told them what her thinking was when writing her will and why she made the decisions she did. It took courage, but doing this significantly reduced any possible strife that might have developed in the step-family after she died.

Chapter 7
Where Are You Going?

"The best way to predict the future is to create it."

PETER DRUCKER

Many people hope that their retired years will be the best in their lives; they say they want to "finish well" and not just give up or fade away. Most people succeed at doing this, especially if they have planned well. Others have hopes, but have not planned for how to fulfill them. What have you done to create the retirement you want? In this chapter, we will look at what you need to do now.

Exercise 1
What, from the Past, Do You
Want to Build into Your Future Life?

1. Review your answers to the exercises in Chapter 4 and write down here the features of your life that you want to make sure will continue into your future. What are the things that you have liked or valued about your life in the past and would be very sad to lose in the future? What does your faith or religion or personal beliefs of any sort suggest to you about your life in retirement? What personal priorities might you have that need to be included in your future life for you to feel satisfied? What passions have you had, fulfilled or unfulfilled, that you

want to keep alive in your future? Where do you want to put your life energy in the future so that, at the end of your life, you will say, "Yes, that was good. I am glad I did that." Write down your thoughts now.

2. What recent discoveries have you had about your life in just the last few years? What have you learned about yourself, your partner, or your family that you did not realize or know before? What have your children or grandchildren taught you about yourself or life in general in just the last few years? What do they say about your life in retirement? What impact does that have on you? Although they may now be dead, what do you think your parents would say about your life in retirement? If they are not dead, could you ask them about their views of retirement in general, and yours in particular? How do their thoughts and feelings relate to yours? How do your plans for retirement relate to your life with your family – with either elderly parents or your own children and grandchildren? How will your position in the family change in the future?

3. What parts of retirement do you think you will like the least? Can you think of ways that you could guard against this? If you tend to be a "worrier," how might that affect your life in retirement? Do you foresee any possible role changes between you and your partner? What sort of issues might arise between you as you learn to deal with new daily schedules that don't involve one or both of you going off to work each day?

4. Taking into account any discoveries or understandings you developed about yourself in Chapter 4, what generalizations would you like to make about your life in the future? What do you think, in general, should be your role in society? In what ways are you, or would you like to be giving to the next generation? At the time of your death, what would you like to be able to say about your life generally and especially your life in retirement?

5. Summarize your thoughts in a sentence or two that starts: "I want my future life to be…." This sentence could be a statement of what your future lifestyle might be. It could be "I want a life of leisure;" "I want to spend my remaining years in volunteer work;" or "develop a second career;" or "engage in continuing education;" or "hike in the Andes," or whatever stands out for you.

6. Discuss all that you have written above with your partner. As with previous exercises, attempt to help each other think about your future with questions that stimulate further thoughtfulness. One major danger in these discussions is to start thinking about how your partner's hopes and plans affect you. If you do this, you may become reactive and evaluative and not be a resource to your partner. Attempt only to be a good friend who is quite interested in how your partner would like his or her life to go. Dealing with what might become divergent dreams for the future can come later in this process.

Exercise 2
Your Vision Statement for Your Future

Write a vision statement for your life in the future. In about a paragraph, say something about who you are and how you want to live your life in the future. The retired life offers us many options for the directions we can take; the vision statement will be your guiding principle. It will help you to make decisions about what direction to take at particular crossroads that may offer many attractive options when you can choose only one. Of course, you may always revise your vision statement at some future time. Discuss this statement with your partner.

Exercise 3
Imagining Your Timeline for the Future

Take a clean sheet of paper, turn it sideways and, as with the timeline you did in Chapter 4, draw a time line that charts how you imagine your future might develop. On the left side of the paper write "Present," and on the right side "Death." Have the line ascend or descend as you imagine how your life might go, showing what you think now might be the highs and lows of life in the future.

Unlike the exercises in Chapter 4, which are based on the actual life you lived, this time line is a totally imaginary process. None of us knows what will happen in our future. However, we can attempt to take it in a particular direction. We can have intentions for our life that we put more or less energy into fulfilling. As the Drucker quote above says, "the best way to predict the future is to create it." As you move into your future life, what signposts will indicate, "Yes, here I have arrived at my intended goal." For example, you might insert that four years into retirement, you "will have become proficient in speaking Spanish."

One way to think about how to divide the line would be your "Good Years," and your "Declining Years." Or you may see your life only getting better and better and such a distinction would not fit. As one example, Ron thought (when he turned 50) that his declining years (physically) would begin at age 70. Having now passed that point, and still being very active physically, he is thinking the big decline will begin somewhere in his 80s. In those years, he imagines that he and Lois will no longer take major trips on their own, but will travel with groups for seniors and have arrangements made for them by the group organizers. He imagines also that he will do cruises, as a form of travel, since they involve less effort. But who knows? Maybe that time will not come until his 90s. He will not mind revising his time line.

This is to say that what we imagine to be our future could be quite wrong, but we can begin making plans for what we imagine. Some people do have a genuine difficulty imagining their future in any sense. Ron once asked a 63-year-old client about his future goals, especially after retirement at age 65. The client said, "You know, I really can't imagine my life after retirement at all. I just have no images." Two years later, Ron heard that the client, within weeks of his retirement, had a heart attack and died.

If you currently have some expectations about what you want to accomplish in your retired life (move to Florida, write a book, travel the world, start a business, earn a degree), insert them on your time line at the point you want to either initiate or accomplish them. While it may sound gruesome, most people have given some passing thought to how they might die. You can include how you imagine your dying process going. Discuss your imagined time line with your partner.

Exercise 4
Brainstorming Ideas for Future Activities and Setting Priorities

1. Make a list, in no particular order, of all of the places you would like to visit, things you would like do, and experiences you would like to have in the future. This would be like your personal bucket list. For example, one thing Ron wrote was "live in a ski resort for a year." Lois wrote, "live on an island for a year."

Attempt to put as many things on this list as you can. Do not be guided by some sort of self-censoring that is saying in your head, "No, no; that is not possible or realistic." Even if it sounds "wild and crazy" but appealing, write it down. Include everything you can possibly think of and let yourself dream; do not be held back by what you think is not possible either financially, physically, or emotionally. For example, one friend loved being around boats. He couldn't afford to own the kind of boat he wanted, but decided to seek a sales job with a boat vendor. He was able to take customers out in some wonderful boats. A woman who had always loved decorating decided to work part-time in a small shop selling decorator items; this led her to offering interior design consulting services.

2. Look over this list and write your answers to the following.

    a. What beliefs and values do you have about time and money that would affect whether you would actually do these things or not?

    b. Are these beliefs and values things that you really want to live your life by in the future? Do they inhibit or enable your hopes for the future? If your beliefs and values were different, are there things that you considered putting on the list but did not, that you would now add to the list?

3. Look at your list. How does it compare with what you wrote about yourself in Exercises 1 and 2 above? If they differ, which approach to your life is more accurate? Sometimes, in Exercises 1 and 2, people write down how they think they "should" live their life, and in this exercise, how they would like to live their life. Granted that the questions are different, there ought to be some correspondence between the two exercises. What adjustments, if any, do you have to make to bring these two exercises closer together? Make this list as comprehensive as possible. Put the items from your list into these categories:

    ♦ Most important (what you definitely want to accomplish)

    ♦ Fairly important (what you would like to have for a satisfying life)

    ♦ Least important (would be nice someday....)

Within the above categories, re-order the items into "priority items" and "to be done some other time." Save that list to review in a few years to see if they are still of interest.

4. After you have selected your top priorities, try them on emotionally. What do they feel like? Do these things accurately portray what you would actually like to do? Would you really enjoy doing them? Would you feel excited and energized? This is where any "should" goals might be questioned. Have you missed something that you had not recognized as you think about these things now? Add it to your list.

5. Discuss this list of priorities and all of your related thoughts with your partner. Be sure to talk also about the things you dropped from your list and things that did not even make the list because "they were not realistic."

   As you discuss your lists with each other, remember that this is just a brainstorming exercise. This is not a time to evaluate each other's ideas or wishes, but to be interested in where the ideas came from, what has made them important, what would be lost if the idea never happened, and specifically how one might fulfill the idea.

6. Discuss with your partner how your priorities listed above might change if your partner was no longer in your life. As difficult as it might be to consider, things do happen. We know of partners who have split at the time of retirement because their visions of the future were so completely different. Or one partner may die suddenly and a whole range of new plans needs to be developed. So, how might your life be different if you were on your own?

Exercise 5
Bringing Together Your Plans As A Couple

1. This is the point to discuss whether and how your wishes for the future can be accomplished together.

For example, we had to decide whether each of us could go along with the other person's desire to "live in a ski resort for a year" and "live on an island for a year." Short of death or separation, how might you each pursue your priorities without the partner's involvement? For example, are separate holiday trips acceptable to each of you? Is there any way to build some of these individually focused goals into your present plans for your life together? Divergent plans for the future do not mean you have to divorce and may even lead to a happier marriage.

a. First, write down any of your ideas that overlap.

b. Now write down items from each other's lists that you could willingly do as a couple. Can some items be done simultaneously rather than serially?

c. List the items that only one of you wants to or could do. Talk about how comfortable that would be for both of you. For example, one partner may want to travel, or go to meditation retreats, or take photography classes and the other does not. It could also happen that one partner prefers to do some things alone, whether or not the other would want to join in. If you are part of a couple who has always done everything together, this is an opportunity to develop a little separateness in your life. Having separate experiences can add to the richness of your joint life.

2. Make three new lists:

   a. Things to be done together:

   b. Things to be done by partner A:

   c. Things to be done by partner B:

Exercise 6
Developing Your Own Timelines

To make it all real, it helps to write down a timeline for when you will start or accomplish the things on your list.

You can use months or years as your basic unit of time. We used a 5-year calendar of months to do ours, though some of the years were just one item for the year: live in a ski resort, for example. Other years had different things for almost every month. Large items such as moving to a retirement community can be broken down into a schedule of when to start exploring places to go, when to start house-hunting, when to move (remembering that these are flexible).

1. Write down together what your plans will be for the coming year(s), actually inserting the items in particular time slots on your calendar, so that the priority items from your brainstorming lists get incorporated. Are there some things that need to be done sooner rather than later, or vice versa?

2. Once you have your plan written down, look at it and see how it feels. Is this really how you want to spend your future years? Have you proposed doing too much or too little? How do the things fit with your lifestyle choices in previous chapters? Are you ready and eager to get started on your plan right away? Do you want to put your energy into doing them as soon as possible? If not, what is that about? Have you been totally honest with yourself up to this point?

3. Discuss your thoughts about all of this and make any modifications in the plan that you want. Are there any ways that one or both of you might sabotage these plans?

Exercise 7
Make It Happen

1. Discuss the steps that need to be taken in order for the plan to be put into action. What particular issues or questions need to be answered and what needs to be researched? What obstacles need to be addressed? What things might distract you from your plan? How will you deal with them?

2. Develop an action plan for each one of your more immediate plans. List what specifically needs to be done, who will do it, and when it will be done by.

Exercise 8
Go Do It! And Enjoy.

RETIREMENT

Chapter 8
The Forms Kit

For some readers, the questions and exercises which are an integral part of this book might be best answered using either pen and paper, or a word processor on a computer.

We have packaged copies of the questions and exercises in two common formats: Microsoft Word (.doc format) and PDF. The package is a compressed "ZIP" file designed to be downloaded to a desktop or laptop computer.

Please write down the link information you see in **bold** text below, then use that in your computer web browser to access and download the kit.

This is the place you can download the free kit of forms, using your computer web browser:

http://self-counsel.com/updates/happy/retire.html

After you download the compressed file, double-click on it to extract the forms kit folder. Open the folder and you will find all the forms, identified by the chapter number in which the questions or exercises occur in this book.

Other Self-Counsel Press Titles
by the Same Author

Birth Order & You

ISBN: 978-1-55180-245-9
$14.95 USD/$18.95 CAD

This book explains how birth order affects the type of person you are, the type of spouse you choose, and the type of employer or employee you make. Between each birth, the family undergoes a reshaping. This updated, new edition includes topics like: how understanding birth order can make you a better parent and partner, and how your birth order affects your career.

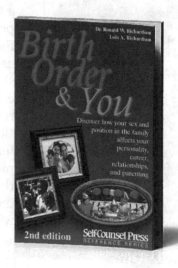

The Authors

Dr. Ronald W. Richardson, BA, MDIV, DMIN, was a marriage counselor and family therapist for over 20 years. He was formerly the Executive Director and Director of Training at the North Shore Counselling Centre in British Columbia. He was also on the faculty of the Pacific Coast Family Therapy Training Association. He is active as a Clinical Member and Approved Supervisor of the American Association for Marriage and Family Therapy and is a Diplomate of the American Association of Pastoral Counselors.

Lois Richardson has an MA in journalism from Syracuse University. She has worked as a newspaper reporter, a freelance writer, and an in-house and freelance editor.

Ron and Lois Richardson co-authored *Birth Order and You* which was first published in 1990 and has continued to sell strongly through two editions and six printings.

Family Ties That Bind

ISBN: 978-1-55180-086-3

$14.95 USD/CAD

Dealing with family relationships in a healthy way is a problem that most people never resolve. This book uses Family of Origin therapy techniques as a basis to improve those relationships and your own sense of self-esteem. Step-by-step exercises show readers how to make contact with "lost" family members, how to interview relatives to develop a clearer picture of how each member fits into the family tree, and how to find different and better ways of dealing with family relationships.

The Author

Dr. Ronald W. Richardson, BA, MDIV, DMIN, has been a marriage counselor and family therapist since 1976. He retired in 1996. He was formerly the Executive Director and Director of Training at the North Shore Counselling Centre in British Columbia. He was also on the faculty of the Pacific Coast Family Therapy Training Association. He is active as a Clinical Member and Approved Supervisor of the American Association for Marriage and Family Therapy and is a Diplomate of the Association for Marriage and Family Therapy and is a Diplomate of the American Association of Pastoral Counselors.

Chapter

1

INTRODUCTION

The more intensively the family has stamped its character upon the child, the more [the child] will tend to feel and see its earlier miniature world again in the bigger world of adult life.

— Carl Gustav Jung

Life in the family of origin (the family a person is born and raised in) is a tremendously powerful experience for everyone. And the impact of that experience is not restricted to childhood. The way we see ourselves, others, and the world is shaped in the setting of our family of origin. The views we develop there stay with us throughout life.

At some point, most of us leave our families of origin physically, but we rarely leave them emotionally. Even if you put an ocean between you and your family of origin, or never return home again, you will continue to re-enact the dynamics of your original family in any new family you establish. The specific content may well be different, of course.

For example, you may do many of the very things your parents did, even though you always swore you wouldn't. No doubt your parents swore the same thing about their parents, who swore the same thing about their parents, back to the first cave man and woman who swore they'd never be the apes their parents were. At times, this decision to be different can take interesting turns.

Example

Annette, a divorced parent with children aged 14, 12, and 9, complained that her parents never liked or approved of what she did. She made a rule for herself as a parent to always praise her children and let them know how much she liked them. To her surprise, her oldest child told her one day, "Mom, the problem with you is you're always telling us how good we are and we can't believe you because we never hear the other side!"

One of the most difficult things in life is to gain emotional separateness from that powerful early family environment and not continually repeat it or react against it.

The purpose of this book is to help you find new ways to deal with that family environment — to have a better life here and now by learning a different way of dealing with your "leftovers" from there and then. If you can look at the unfinished business of your past in an appropriate context — the environment of your family of origin — your present and future experiences in life can be more positive. You can be more in charge of your own life, less defeated by undesirable events, and better able to create for yourself the kind of life you want.

Think about how you feel when you visit or phone your parents. Do you feel or act similarly to the way you did when you were living at home? How long can you last before the old feelings start? Five minutes? An hour? Two days? What happens to you when things start getting tense? If you can last more than three days before acting or feeling like a 13-year-old again, you probably don't need this book. Most adults, however, tend to act in ways they wish were different. Some attempt to fit in as peacefully as possible. They deny their own feelings, do what their parents want, and don't rock the boat.

Others make a point of being the opposite of what their parents want and expect. They are perpetual rebels.

Some try to show their parents how they failed as parents and work on improving them. Many just have as little to do with family as possible. They are emotionally distant and rarely visit or communicate with their families.

All of these ways of relating bear testimony to the power of our families in our lives. Most of us have not learned how to be close to these significant people while continuing to feel like our own persons. We find ourselves reacting to them, rather than doing what would make sense to us in our most objective moments. Yet, until you can be an independent adult with your family, it is unlikely you can be this way with anyone else in an intimate relationship.

The same issues end up getting dumped into new intimate relationships: marriage (legal or common-law, same-sex or opposite-sex), children, work, friendships. The extent to which a satisfying adult life can be established is dependent upon how well you learn to deal with these forces in your family of origin.

One way to do this is through family of origin work. The goal of this work is to change your experience of yourself in your family of origin and, by extension, in your present relationships.

None of us really has a choice about whether to deal with our families or not. Even choosing not to deal with them is a way of dealing with them. You can't be free of your early experiences by denying their significance or ignoring them. Your early experiences are bound to repeat in your present life with different characters and in different contexts.

Doing family of origin work is one way to begin changing this self-defeating pattern. Some people do this work with a counselor, or a family therapist, but you can also do it on your own. In fact, people were using this approach long before family therapists started taking credit for it. A natural part of becoming a mature adult is to reassess the earlier relationships with family and make adjustments in them.

Doing family of origin work requires an understanding of how families function. Chapters 2 to 7 will help you with this. Those chapters discuss specific family dynamics that you will want to examine in your own situation. Throughout these chapters are questions and exercises for you to think about and do. You don't have to sit down and write out answers to the questions, but you will benefit most if you read each one carefully and let it simmer in your mind as you read further. Do the exercises that make sense to you in your situation and that you feel comfortable with.

Understanding the concepts and being able to identify the dynamics at work in your family are only the first steps. This book is not intended to provide insight only into your family. For that insight to be meaningful, you will have to change your behavior and way of being in your family of origin. Chapter 8 gives you the instructions for doing the practical work. But don't cheat and skip straight to that chapter; it won't make a lot of sense unless you know something about the theory that comes first. Take your time and be patient. Once you have waded through all the theory, you will be amazed at how well and simply it all fits together.

Even those who have been out of touch with their families for years can do this work; old relationships can be renewed. If your parents are dead, friends or relatives can be contacted for information about your childhood environment.

People of any age can and do use this method for changing themselves, although it is easiest for those who are at least in their late twenties.

Younger people are often still trying to get away physically and can't yet handle the stickier emotional separation. However, no matter what your age, dealing with your family of origin can be difficult, and you may find it easier if you have some support. If you are fortunate enough to know a therapist who is familiar with family of origin therapy, you would do well to use his or her services. Because family of origin work requires you to do all the work, these therapists usually call themselves coaches. In fact, any good listener who can provide the support you need and ask appropriate questions can be this kind of coach. Sometimes a group of friends can provide this for each other in regular meetings set up for this purpose.

A spouse or lover does not make a good coach. Even the best of them find it extremely difficult to remain neutral about family matters. Your spouse's involvement can only complicate things for you. Your coach must be able to ask you a lot of questions to help you begin to think differently about your family. Spouses are more likely to tell you what to think despite their best intentions.

You also won't get very far with this work if you do it with someone (spouse or therapist) who believes that your parents are to blame for all your problems. You'll just end up feeling justified for your anger or hurt, or whatever your feelings are toward your family. The point is for you to change — and you must do that by looking at your family in a different light.

One warning: Some people, who are deeply troubled or come from families with severe emotional problems or a history of sexual abuse, should not attempt to do this work without professional help. However, most average people with only the normal complement of problems can do this work without involving a third party.